UNBELIEVABLE!

34 AMAZING FACTS ABOUT MUMMIES

Hannah Gramson

Lerner Publications ◆ Minneapolis

Lerner Publications Company
An imprint of Lerner Publishing Group, Inc.
241 First Avenue North
Minneapolis, MN 55401 USA

For reading levels and more information, look up this title at www.lernerbooks.com.

Main body text set in ITC Franklin Gothic Std.
Typeface provided by Adobe Systems.

Editor: Elena Mai **Designer:** Mary Ross **Photo Editor:** Lucien Brinkley

Library of Congress Cataloging-in-Publication Data

Names: Gramson, Hannah author
Title: 34 amazing facts about mummies / Hannah Gramson.
Other titles: Thirty-four amazing facts about mummies
Description: Minneapolis, MN : Lerner Publications, [2026] | Series: Unbelievable! (updog books) | Includes bibliographical references and index. | Audience: Ages 8–11 | Audience: Grades 2–3 | Summary: "Mummies were discovered in many parts of the world, including ancient Egypt. Readers will learn amazing facts about how mummies were made, famous mummies, and the tombs where mummies were buried in this fun book"— Provided by publisher.
Identifiers: LCCN 2025011233 (print) | LCCN 2025011234 (ebook) | ISBN 9798765689745 library binding | ISBN 9798348029500 paperback | ISBN 9798765699621 epub
Subjects: LCSH: Mummies—Juvenile literature
Classification: LCC GN293 .G77 2026 (print) | LCC GN293 (ebook) | DDC 393/.3—dc23/eng/20250425

LC record available at https://lccn.loc.gov/2025011233
LC ebook record available at https://lccn.loc.gov/2025011234

Manufactured in the United States of America
1-1012513-54842-5/21/2025

Table of Contents

The Afterlife 4

Making a Mummy 10

List Break! 16

Inside a Tomb 18

Royal Mummies 24

Glossary 30

Check It Out! 31

Index 32

THE AFTERLIFE

Ancient Egyptians were one of the many ancient cultures that made mummies.

They made mummies for over three thousand years.

In that time, the Egyptians made over seventy million mummies.

Ancient Egyptians believed in an afterlife.

They thought a person's spirit could live on after death.

But only if their body was protected from breaking down.

Up Next!

CUT AND WRAP.

MAKING A MUMMY

The first step to creating a mummy was removing the organs.

Jars for mummy organs

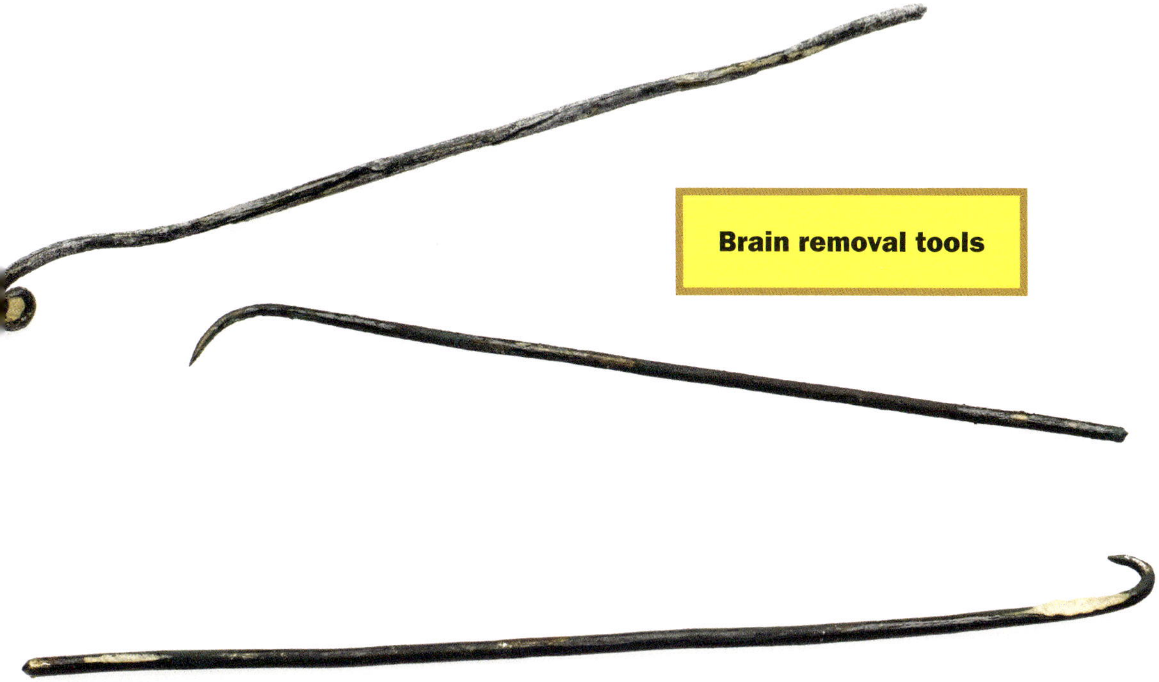

Brain removal tools

The brain was removed through the nose. Then it was thrown away!

Only the heart was left in the body. Other organs were placed in jars.

Mummy heart

The body was left covered in salt for days. This dried it out.

Then it was wrapped in hundreds of yards of cloth strips.

All of this took up to seventy days.

LIST BREAK!

Mummies have been found all over the world. Here are the top five countries where mummies were found.

1. Egypt
2. Italy
3. Peru
4. Chile
5. China

A mummy from China

Ramesses the Great

Who are the most famous mummies of Egypt?

1. King Tut
2. Hatshepsut
3. Ramesses the Great
4. Seti I
5. Amenhotep III

Up Next!

BURYING THE DEAD.

INSIDE A TOMB

Most mummies were buried in tombs.

Board games were buried in tombs.

They were buried with things people thought they would need in the afterlife.

A game in King Tut's tomb

Clothes, furniture, and other objects were buried in tombs.

One Egyptian mummy was found buried with a 144-foot (44 m) boat.

Ancient Egyptian bottles and bowls

Some mummies were even buried with food.

One famous mummy's tomb had over one hundred baskets of food inside.

Up Next!

PHARAOHS.

ROYAL MUMMIES

Some pharaohs were put in tombs under huge pyramids.

The most famous royal tomb belongs to King Tut.

It was found in 1922 in Egypt.

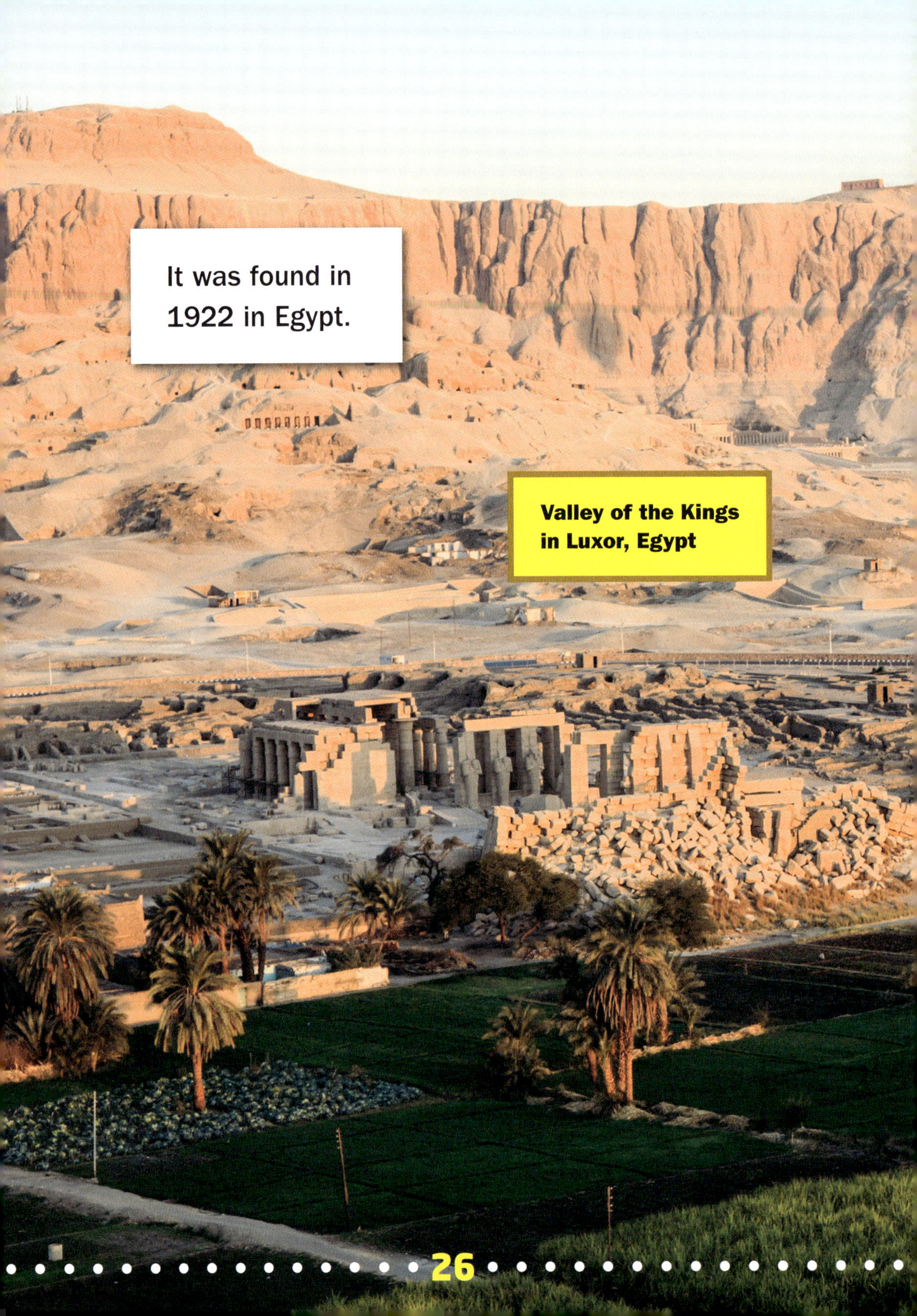

Valley of the Kings in Luxor, Egypt

King Tut was buried with over five thousand treasures.

His coffin was made of solid gold!

Mummies can be seen in many museums around the world.

Glossary

afterlife: a life after death

ancient: of or relating to a period of time long ago

organ: a body part made up of tissue, such as the heart or brain

pharaoh: a ruler in ancient Egypt

tomb: a place built for the dead

Check It Out!

Britannica Kids: Ancient Egypt
https://kids.britannica.com/kids/article/ancient-Egypt/353087

Carlson-Berne, Emma. *Mummies Around the World*. Lerner Publications, 2024.

Gleason, Carrie. *Guide to Mummies*. Crabtree, 2023.

Markovics, Joyce. *Animal Mummies*. Cherry Lake, 2021.

National Geographic Kids: The Discovery of King Tut's Tomb
https://kids.nationalgeographic.com/history/article/the-discovery-of-king-tuts-tomb

TIME for Kids: Egyptian Mummies
https://www.timeforkids.com/k1/egyptian-mummies/

Index

afterlife, 8, 19
ancient Egypt, 4, 6–7

King Tut, 17, 25, 27

organs, 10–12

tombs, 18, 24–25

Photo Acknowledgments

Image credits: Funds from various donors, 1886/The Metropolitan Museum of Art, New York, Open Access, pp. 3, 17 (bottom); Wolfgang Kaehler/Alamy, p. 4; Images & Stories/Alamy, p. 5; © The Trustees of the British Museum, p. 6; RhondaSuka/Getty Images, p. 7; Rogers Fund, 1932/The Metropolitan Museum of Art, New York, Open Access, p. 8; PRISMA ARCHIVO/Alamy, pp. 9, 22; lego 19861111/Shutterstock, p. 10; Wellcome Images (CC-BY-4.0), p. 11; Isidro Albert, Gonzálvez Luis M., Huber Beatrice/Mummified Heart of an Ancient Egyptian, Revista Española de Cardiología (English Edition), p. 12; Diego Jesus Sanchez Torres/Alamy, p. 13; Lanmas/Alamy, pp. 14–15, 23; Iain Masterton/Alamy, p. 16; Franck Legros/Alamy, p. 17 (top); Randa G/Shutterstock, p. 18; Purchase, Edward S. Harkness Gift, 1926 (26.7.1287a-k): Gift of Lord Carnarvon, 2012 (2012.508)/The Metropolitan Museum of Art, New York, Open Access, p. 19; Courtesy of Wikimedia Commons (CC BY-SA 4.0), p. 20; TJ Brown/Shutterstock, p. 21; Shanna Baker/Getty Images, p. 24; Sergii Figurnyi/Shutterstock, p. 25; takepicsforfun/Getty Images, p. 26; Caroline Léna Becker (CC0 1.0), p. 27; Karl Kost/Alamy, p. 28; Panther Media GmbH/Alamy, p. 29.

Cover: Brandon Rosenblum/Getty Images.